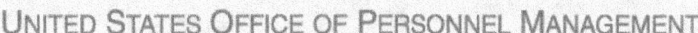
UNITED STATES OFFICE OF PERSONNEL MANAGEMENT

I0410941

Guide to Telework
in the
Federal Government

April 2011

a New Day for Federal Service

Table of Contents

INTRODUCTION AND BACKGROUND

Introduction

The Federal Government is a leader in the use of innovative workplace flexibilities, including telework. In March 2010, President Obama hosted a <u>White House Forum</u> on flexibilities, emphasizing their vital role in recruiting and retaining the best and brightest workers and maximizing their effectiveness. Congress passed the Telework Enhancement Act of 2010 to catalyze expansion.

Federal telework programs are established primarily to meet agency mission and operational needs. Telework saves money by helping government reduce real estate and energy costs and promote management efficiencies; makes us more resilient in severe weather and other emergencies; improves the quality of employee work-life; and increases employment opportunities for persons with disabilities.

Advances in information technology have paved the way for increased telework. However, telework is not a new concept and is not necessarily dependent on the use of technology. The key is for managers and employees to clearly define the work expectations and objectives, and then to give employees the tools and flexibility needed to get the job done.

This *Guide to Telework in the Federal Government* outlines practical information to assist Federal agencies, managers, supervisors, Telework Managing Officers[1], other staff responsible for implementing telework, and employees. Perhaps you are an employee who would like to know more about telework. Maybe you manage or supervise teleworking staff and hope to develop a better understanding of the day-to-day aspects of this important flexibility. You may be a Telework Managing Officer or another staff member tasked with oversight or operational responsibilities related to the telework program at your agency. Perhaps you are a labor representative with a need to know the finer points of a great telework program. If any of these describe your situation, then this *Guide* is for you.

Legislative Background

For many years, laws addressing telework (under various names – "work at home," "flexible work," "telecommuting," etc.) have been in effect for Federal employees. The initial legislative mandate for telework was established in 2000 (<u>§ 359 of Public Law 106-346</u>). This law states that "[e]ach executive agency shall establish a policy under which eligible employees of the agency may participate in telecommuting to the maximum extent possible without diminished employee performance." Associated language in the conference report for this legislation expanded on that requirement where it said that "[e]ach agency participating in the program shall develop criteria to be used in implementing such a policy and ensure that managerial, logistical, organizational, or other barriers to full implementation and successful functioning of the policy are removed. Each agency should also provide for adequate administrative, human resources, technical, and logistical support for carrying out the policy."

---

[1] A senior-level official at each agency responsible and accountable for policy development and implementation related to the agency's telework program.

Further legislation (Public Law 108-199, Division B, § 627 of January 23, 2004, and Public Law 108-447, Division B, § 622 of December 8, 2004) followed this mandate with directives to certain agencies to increase telework participation in the workforce by specified amounts.

In response to the original congressional mandate, the Office of Personnel Management (OPM) began to survey Federal agencies about telework in 2000. By means of the annual "Call for Telework Data," OPM collaborates with Federal agencies to collect information about individual agency telework programs, including participation rates. The analysis of that data is presented in the yearly Status of Telework in the Federal Government Report to the Congress, published annually since 2002. You may review these reports for historical and background information on Federal telework at the central website at www.telework.gov.

The Telework Enhancement Act of 2010 (the Act), was signed into law on December 9, 2010. The passage and signing of this legislation (Public Law 111-292) was a significant milestone in the history of Federal telework. The Act is a key factor in the Federal Government's ability to achieve greater flexibility in managing its workforce through the use of telework. The law specifies roles, responsibilities and expectations for all Federal executive agencies with regard to telework policies; employee eligibility and participation; program implementation; and reporting. It also assigns specific duties to OPM; General Services Administration (GSA); Office of Management and Budget (OMB); Department of Homeland Security (DHS), including the Federal Emergency Management Agency (FEMA); National Archives and Records Administration (NARA); and others. The specific agencies named in the Act are charged with directing overall policy and providing policy guidance to Federal executive agencies on an ongoing basis. The Act established baseline expectations for the Federal telework program and agencies have been diligent to implement its requirements seamlessly and effectively.

What is Telework?

Definition

The official definition of "telework" can be found in the Telework Enhancement Act of 2010 (the Act): "[t]he term 'telework' or 'teleworking' refers to a work flexibility arrangement under which an employee performs the duties and responsibilities of such employee's position, and other authorized activities, from an approved worksite other than the location from which the employee would otherwise work."

In practice, "telework" is a work arrangement that allows an employee to perform work, during any part of regular, paid hours, at an approved alternative worksite (e.g., home, telework center). This definition of telework includes what is generally referred to as remote work but does not include any part of work done while on official travel or mobile work.

REMOTE: In the past, agencies have sometimes used this term to describe a work arrangement in which the employee resides and works at a location beyond the local commuting area of the employing organization's worksite or to describe a full-time telework arrangement. For reporting purposes, these employees should be included as teleworkers.

MOBILE: Work which is characterized by routine and regular travel to conduct work in customer or other worksites as opposed to a single authorized alternative worksite. Examples of mobile work include site audits, site inspections, investigations, property management, and work performed while commuting, traveling between worksites, or on Temporary Duty (TDY).

You may also be familiar with the terms "telecommuting" and "flexible workplace" and both are sometimes used to describe what we now generally refer to as "telework." While "remote" and "mobile" work are also terms that are sometimes used as synonyms for telework, they tend to operate differently than telework as is apparent in the detailed operational definition.

For consistency, OPM recommends that all agencies use the term "telework" for reporting purposes and for all other activities related to policy and legislation, as defined in the Act.

Types of Telework Arrangements

Generally speaking, there are two types of telework; 1) routine telework in which telework occurs as part of an ongoing, regular schedule and 2) situational telework that is approved on a case-by-case basis, where the hours worked were NOT part of a previously approved, ongoing and regular telework schedule. Examples of situational telework include telework as a result of inclement weather, doctor appointment, or special work assignments, and is sometimes also referred to as situational, episodic, intermittent, unscheduled, or ad-hoc telework. It is important to note that **any employee who wishes to telework** (regardless of which type) **must first successfully complete an interactive telework training program** provided by the agency and **must enter into a written agreement with his/her supervisor**. OPM recommends that supervisors and managers of teleworking employees complete telework training.

When one typically refers to a "teleworker," the picture that most often comes to mind is the first type described above, i.e., someone who is approved to telework on a schedule that is regular and recurring, most often on an agreed-upon day or days during a bi-weekly pay period (e.g., someone teleworks "every Wednesday" or "every Tuesday and Thursday"). The specific days that are regularly scheduled for telework are spelled out in a written telework agreement between the employee and that employee's supervisor.

There are many different scenarios in which an employee can be approved for telework under the second type described above, i.e., situational, episodic, or ad-hoc. Since every employee that is eligible to telework has formally received training and entered into a written telework agreement, these employees may be approved by their supervisors to telework on a case-by-case basis as the need arises. Examples include but are not limited to the following: 1) an employee has a short-term need for uninterrupted time to complete work on a complex project or report; 2) an employee is recovering from illness or an injury and is temporarily unable to physically report to the traditional office; and 3) an employee receives word of an OPM announcement on the status of Federal Government operations in the Washington, DC, area due to inclement weather as "Open with Option for Unscheduled Leave or Unscheduled Telework," and notifies her/his supervisor that s/he would like to opt for unscheduled telework that day.

Note that by definition, "unscheduled telework" is a specific form of situational or ad-hoc telework. Agencies and employees are encouraged to consult the OPM publication, *Washington, DC, Area Dismissal and Closure Procedures*, for answers to questions about "unscheduled telework" during dismissal or closure situations.

Telework arrangements in the Federal Government may be full-time or part-time. Part-time schedules are more common. As with most aspects of the telework program, Federal agencies have discretion to define the types of arrangements and parameters for participation within their telework policies and telework agreements. In exercising this discretion, agencies should consider individual employee needs while ensuring that telework does not diminish employee performance or agency operations. There is more guidance on policies and agreements later in this document.

While some agencies do allow full-time telework, it is not the norm. In fact, the Act specifically identifies the following categories of part-time participation and requires that agencies report on the specific number of employees each year that telework:

➤ 3 or more days per pay period (denotes a bi-weekly pay period)
➤ 1 or 2 days per pay period
➤ once per month
➤ on an occasional, episodic, or short-term basis (i.e., situational telework such as ad-hoc or unscheduled telework as described above).

TELEWORK GUIDANCE BY AUDIENCE

Federal Agencies/Telework Managing Officers

This segment provides guidance to Federal agencies regarding their responsibilities under the Act to establish and implement telework programs. By extension, it offers practical information to the agency's designated Telework Managing Officer (TMO), by law each agency's primary point of contact to OPM on telework matters.

Telework Fundamentals

Federal law regarding telework applies to **all employees of Federal executive agencies** (agencies). Subject to the limitations described in the law and as defined by individual agency telework policies and applicable collective bargaining agreements, employees may participate in telework regardless of the geographic location where they work (i.e., domestic or overseas).

It is important to understand that **telework is not an employee right**, i.e., Federal law requires agencies to establish telework programs but does not give individual employees a legal right to telework. Also, **telework may not be used as a substitute for dependent care**. That being said, it is clear that the intent of the laws on telework is to encourage agencies to allow employee participation in the telework program to the maximum extent possible without diminished employee performance. Agencies should keep this in mind when developing telework policies and agreements, and when considering formal requests from employees to telework. The Act recognized this intent when it required agencies by June 7, 2011 (i.e., 180 days from enactment of the law) to "establish a policy under which eligible employees of the agency may be authorized to telework;" to "determine the eligibility for all employees of the agency to participate in telework;" and to "notify all employees of the agency of their eligibility to telework."

Another important factor to remember is that **employee participation in telework is voluntary**.[2] The Act does not mandate telework or promote telework for its own sake. Instead, it asks agencies to implement telework as a workplace flexibility that assists the agency to maintain continuity of operations and reduce management costs while also improving Federal employees' ability to balance their work and life commitments. The Act encourages an increase in the use of telework, but only for employees who choose to do so. This means that an agency may not compel an employee to telework, even if the duties of the position make that employee "telework eligible."

In the final analysis, **telework is primarily an arrangement established to facilitate the accomplishment of work**. While employees and agencies alike enjoy positive outcomes resulting from telework, agencies retain both the discretion and the obligation to determine employee eligibility for telework subject to business-related, operational needs and the limitations described in the Act.

---

[2] Although entering into the telework arrangement is voluntary, once the employee is under such an arrangement, he or she may be required to telework outside of his or her normal telework schedule in the case of a temporary emergency situation if that understanding has been clearly communicated by the agency to the teleworking employee in the written telework agreement (see the appropriate section below).

Agency Roles and Responsibilities

Of all the legislation to date, the Act provides the most comprehensive view of what is expected of Federal agencies with regard to telework. All Federal executive agencies are responsible to fulfill several requirements identified in the Act. Several specific agencies have additional duties to provide oversight, guidance and overall support with the implementation of telework programs.

❖ **Every Federal Executive agency** will:

➢ establish a policy under which eligible employees may be authorized to telework

➢ determine employee eligibility to participate in telework

➢ notify all employees of their eligibility to telework

➢ incorporate telework into Continuity of Operations (COOP) plans

➢ ensure that each eligible employee authorized to telework enters into a written telework agreement with his/her supervisor

➢ ensure that an interactive telework training program is provided to eligible employees and their managers and that the program is successfully completed by employees prior to entering into a written telework agreement

➢ designate a TMO to serve as the primary point of contact with OPM on telework matters on behalf of the agency

➢ while developing telework policies, consult with OPM as needed for policy guidance in various areas such as performance management, pay and leave, recruitment and retention, etc.

When fulfilling the requirements of the Act, Federal agencies will:

➢ allow pre-decisional involvement on development of telework policies with employee representatives to the fullest extent practicable as provided in Executive Order 13522

➢ ensure that appropriate collective bargaining obligations are satisfied with employee representatives on agency telework policies.

The Act required agencies to fulfill specific provisions of the law no later than 180 days from enactment (June 7, 2011). Other requirements are ongoing as new employees come on board and policies and agreements are routinely reviewed and modified over time.

❖ **OPM** shall:

➢ provide consultation, policy and policy guidance to the agencies on telework in the areas of pay and leave; agency closure; performance management; official worksite; recruitment and retention; and accommodations for persons with disabilities

➢ assist each agency in establishing appropriate qualitative and quantitative measures and teleworking goals

- consult with the **General Services Administration (GSA)** on policy and policy guidance for telework in the areas of telework centers, travel, technology, equipment and dependent care

- consult with the **Federal Emergency Management Agency (FEMA)** on policy and policy guidance for telework in the areas of continuation of operations and long-term emergencies

- consult with the **National Archives and Records Administration (NARA)** on policy and policy guidance for telework in the areas of efficient and effective records management; and preservation of records, including Presidential and Vice-Presidential records.

OPM is also responsible for maintaining a central telework website that includes telework links, announcements, and guidance developed by OPM or submitted by FEMA and GSA (OPM is required to post FEMA and GSA guidance no later than 10 business days from receiving it). This central website may be accessed at www.telework.gov. OPM and GSA have traditionally worked together to support telework in the Federal Government. The website at www.telework.gov is the result of an ongoing collaboration, between OPM and GSA, to provide timely and practical information to agencies, managers, employees and other interested parties to effectively implement telework programs and arrangements, as well as information of interest to the general public. OPM and GSA also work directly with TMOs at each agency to provide guidance and assistance as needed.

OPM, in collaboration with each agency, is required to compile and submit an annual report on the telework programs of each agency, beginning with the first report submitted 18 months after enactment of the law (June 2012), and on a yearly basis thereafter. The initial report after the law's enactment will establish the new baseline for the annual *Status of Telework in the Federal Government Report to the Congress*. OPM is also tasked with researching the utilization of telework by public and private sector entities that identify best practices and recommendations for the Federal government. Finally, the law directed OPM to review the outcomes associated with an increase in telework, including the effects of telework on energy consumption, job creation and availability, urban transportation patterns, and the ability to anticipate the dispersal of work during periods of emergency, and to make findings available to the public.

- ❖ **OMB** is required to:

  - consult with the **Department of Homeland Security (DHS)** and the **National Institute of Standards and Technology (NIST)**, to issue guidelines to ensure the adequacy of information and security protections for information and information systems used while teleworking (with guidelines to be completed by June 7, 2011 - 180 days from enactment of the law)

  - issue policy guidance requiring each agency, when purchasing computer systems, to purchase systems that enable and support telework, unless the agency head determines that there is a mission-specific reason not to do so (with guidance to be completed by April 8, 2011 – 120 days from the law's enactment).

Telework Policies

The Act requires each agency to:

1. establish a telework policy under which eligible employees of the agency may be authorized to telework
2. determine the eligibility for all employees of the agency to participate in telework
3. notify all employees of the agency of their eligibility to telework.

The Act directs agencies to fulfill these requirements no later than 180 days from enactment of the law (June 7, 2011). Agency policies also should describe a reasonable timeframe in which newly hired employees of the agency will be notified of their eligibility to telework.

Section 359 of Public Law 106-346 (October 23, 2000), stated that "[e]ach executive agency shall establish a policy under which eligible employees of the agency may participate in telecommuting to the maximum extent possible without diminished employee performance." Therefore, the law required executive agencies to have a telework policy in place long before the passage of the Act (Public Law 111-292). However, the Act expanded upon and strengthened the Federal Government's commitment to the telework program. Accordingly, each agency was required to carefully review and revise its existing telework policy by June 7, 2011, to ensure compliance with the requirements of the Act.

For example, prior legislation did not offer details on the elements needed to establish a telework program at an agency (e.g., creating telework agreements) or how to go about implementing the day-to-day operational aspects of telework. The Act provided several clarifying criteria and agencies incorporated the changes into their existing policies. Agencies should plan to review their telework policies from time to time to ensure consistency with any future changes or modifications to telework legislation.

Agencies also should allow pre-decisional involvement to the fullest extent practicable as provided in Executive Order 13522 and satisfy collective bargaining obligations by working with labor when developing their telework polices and agreements.

In 2009-2010, OPM collaborated with agencies to perform a thorough review of their individual telework policies. The criteria by which policies were evaluated by OPM were derived from a thorough review of current research and best practices in telework, conducted by an interagency group of Federal telework experts. At the conclusion of the review, OPM provided specific feedback to agencies recommending revisions to their policies, and agencies followed through with implementation. The work jointly accomplished at that time laid a firm foundation for the development of sound telework policies as required by the Act.

There is no requirement in the Act that an agency submit its telework policy to OPM for its review or to determine compliance with the law. What the Act *does require* is that each executive agency "consult with the Office of Personnel Management in developing telework policies." The law further explains that OPM shall "provide policy and policy guidance for telework in the areas of pay and leave, agency closure, performance management, official worksite, recruitment and retention, and accommodations for employees with disabilities." Additionally, OPM will "assist each agency in establishing appropriate qualitative and quantitative measures and teleworking goals." OPM provides consultation by means of telework guidance and information offered on the central website at www.telework.gov (including this *Guide*) and at regularly-scheduled OPM-sponsored forums with TMOs in the course of the year.

A well-written telework policy is the foundation for a good telework program. For any agencies that wish to revisit or strengthen their telework policies, below are specific criteria that should be included in an effective policy:

There are two main objectives to be met if you are to have an effective telework policy:

1. The policy should be written in such a way that it can be clearly understood and easily used.

2. The policy should incorporate content fundamental to the development and support of an effective telework program.

❖ CLARITY AND USABILITY

Policies should:

➢ use concrete, familiar words and not jargon, unexplained abbreviations, or other difficult terminology (i.e., keep your "end-users" in mind, many of whom may be unfamiliar with telework)

➢ avoid ambiguous terms and redundancies

➢ be organized logically (e.g., in preparing the various sections, do not skip around from topic to topic but instead organize the material by category for ease of reference)

➢ be designed and written to serve as a useful, practical resource to employees, managers, supervisors of teleworkers, TMOs, telework coordinators, Human Resource Specialists, exclusive employee representatives, and any other staff with a need to know about the agency's telework program.

❖ CONTENT FUNDAMENTAL TO DEVELOP AND SUPPORT A TELEWORK PROGRAM

The policy should include content critical to the success of a telework program. Generally, content should cover issues related to: a) program implementation (i.e., content that supports effective program development), b) participant responsibilities (i.e., content that defines the roles and responsibilities of various participants in telework such as employees, managers, supervisors, and TMOs), and c) program operations (content that details the day-to-day activities or information necessary to support program success).

Specifically, with regard to <u>Program Implementation</u>, the telework policy should:

- include a statement of purpose (e.g., that identifies the intended benefits or outcomes of telework such as emergency preparedness, workforce efficiency, quality of work-life balance, cost savings, etc.)

- contain clear definitions of a) telework, b) eligibility, c) official worksite/duty station, and d) alternative worksite/location

- reference governing telework legislation such as Public Law 106-346 and Public Law 111-292 (Telework Enhancement Act of 2010)

- reference citations and appendices when reference is made to internal or external sources such as authorities, documents and related policies. If the telework policy is to be included on a web-based system such as Intranet for employee access, you may wish to include hyperlinks to these references for easier accessibility

- include language that reflects the Act's intent that all employees of the agency meeting the definition of "employee" as defined in Section 2105 of Title 5 of the United States Code are covered by the policy

- state that employee participation in a telework arrangement is voluntary

- emphasize that telework is an arrangement established first and foremost to facilitate the accomplishment of work

- include information about how to identify telework-eligible positions, including how to apply the limitations on participation described in the Act, e.g., identifying any legal bars to permitting an employee to telework, considering the nature of the work to be performed, and assessing whether permitting a particular employee -- or employees in a particular position -- to telework would diminish employee performance or agency operations

- reference agency emergency policies (e.g., pandemics and disasters prompting COOP procedures; dismissal and closure procedures due to weather; etc.) and the expectations that will be imposed upon given employees, with respect to these policies, if an employee enters into a telework arrangement with the agency.

- reference agency information technology (IT) and cybersecurity guidelines

- reference the Federal Employees' Compensation Act (FECA)

- highlight the importance of employee safety while working at alternative worksites

- identify aspects of the employment arrangement that could possibly be modified when an employee participates in telework (e.g., teleworkers may be allowed to begin the work day earlier and end earlier than on those days when they commute)

➢ identify whether full-time telework arrangements are allowable in the agency and if so, aspects of the employment arrangement that could potentially change if an employee teleworks full-time (e.g., could there be consequences to locality pay, benefits, travel, reduction-in-force procedures, etc.).

With regard to Participant Responsibilities, the telework policy should:

➢ define the responsibilities of supervisors and managers of teleworkers

➢ define the responsibilities of teleworking employees

➢ define the responsibilities of TMOs and telework coordinators

➢ emphasize teleworker responsibilities to ensure the arrangement does not have any negative impact on the work of other members of the work group (e.g., co-workers, supervisors)

➢ outline what support, materials, and equipment the agency may provide for teleworkers; what the agency will not provide; and what responsibilities for such may be shared between the agency and the teleworker (e.g., providing laptops, printers, phone, supplies, Internet service, etc.); agencies may wish to consult with their counsel concerning the implications of appropriations law for this subject.

➢ assign clearly-stated responsibilities for record keeping and reporting requirements, not only for the daily operational aspects but also for reporting to OPM in the aggregate each year (e.g., the annual *Status of Telework in the Federal Government Report to the Congress*).

With regard to Program Operations, the telework policy should:

➢ describe procedures for establishing a telework arrangement (e.g., application, approval levels, timeline for approval/denial, training requirements, written agreement, etc.)

➢ note that, with respect to employees covered by a collective bargaining agreement, appeals will be governed by the negotiated grievance procedure (unless this subject is specifically excluded from that procedure by the collective bargaining agreement, in which case the agency grievance procedure would govern) and that, for non-bargaining unit employees, the agency grievance procedure in force would cover appeals from a denial of a request to telework

➢ establish that the performance of teleworkers will be evaluated consistent with the agency's regular performance management system (i.e., teleworkers should be treated the same as non-teleworkers with regard to performance management)

➢ emphasize that teleworkers will receive the same treatment and opportunities as non-teleworkers (e.g., work assignments, awards and recognition, development opportunities, promotions, etc.)

- address expectations regarding communication between employees and supervisors; employees and co-workers; employees and customers/clients; and others. Will it be via telephone, email or a combination? How often should communication take place?

- identify specific agency requirements for training of employees prior to entering into a written telework agreement and beginning to telework

- identify agency expectations regarding telework training for managers and supervisors of teleworkers

- address unexpected contingencies that could impact the telework arrangement. Clearly define expectations of teleworking employees during situations that involve early dismissal, late arrival, or closure of Federal offices to the public. What explicit procedures should be followed when emergency events occur that may involve closure at the official worksite, alternative worksite, etc.? Also describe procedures to be followed in case of illness, recall during a telework day to the official site to meet business-related needs, etc. Will you allow a substitution day for the telework day missed, etc.?

- identify procedures for changing or modifying telework arrangements (e.g., schedules or locations)

- require that the written telework agreement be reviewed at regular intervals as determined by the agency

- describe procedures for termination or withdrawal from a telework agreement; with respect to terminations of telework, note that, for employees covered by a collective bargaining agreement, appeals will be governed by the negotiated grievance procedure (unless this subject is specifically excluded from that procedure by the collective bargaining agreement, in which case the agency grievance procedure would govern) and that, for non-bargaining unit employees, the agency grievance procedure in force would cover appeals.

- include clear and specific requirements for record keeping and reporting, both for individual teleworkers and to keep track of telework in the agency for reporting purposes each year (i.e., annual report to Congress). OPM recommends that the agency describe in the policy the system and workflow being used to capture participation of the various types of telework, i.e., bi-weekly work report, time and attendance system; payroll provider, etc. and provide specific instructions to managers and employees that this information must be carefully and consistently collected either manually or electronically for reporting purposes

- include clear and specific requirements for evaluation of the telework program, both for the individual teleworker and for the agency in general.

Eligibility and Participation

Agencies have discretion to make their own eligibility determinations for employees subject to operational needs while considering the specific requirements described in the Act. In making these decisions, individual agencies are in the best position to define what it means to "ensure that telework does not diminish employee performance or agency operations." There are a variety of circumstances in each individual agency that relate to position classification, organizational structures and agency mission areas. As a result, it would be impractical and inadvisable for OPM to suggest a Governmentwide "standard" or develop generic language that would imply a "one-size-fits- all" approach to making eligibility determinations and in notifying employees of eligibility. Agencies should take special care to specifically describe eligibility and participation criteria in their telework policies.

Bear in mind that the Act makes a clear distinction between "eligibility" and "participation." To be able to participate in telework, an employee must first be identified as eligible. The Act specifies two categories of employees who may not be deemed eligible under any circumstances: an employee who "has been officially disciplined for being absent without permission for more than 5 days in any calendar year" and an employee who "has been officially disciplined for violations of subpart G of the Standards of Ethical Conduct of Employees of the Executive Branch for reviewing, downloading, or exchanging pornography, including child pornography, on a Federal Government computer or while performing official Federal Government duties [Public Law 111-292, 6502(a)(2)(A)(B)]." Thus, the Act does not establish new eligibility standards; rather, it specifies two conditions that make an employee *in*eligible. As before the signing of the Telework Act, specific determinations for eligibility are left to the discretion of agencies and should reflect agreement with standards established in individual agency policies.

The Act directly prohibits eligibility for telework only in the two narrow instances cited above. However, what does the term "officially disciplined" mean? Also, if an employee has been officially disciplined as described, does this permanently bar that employee from telework or is there a specific time limitation after which the employee may now be considered for telework? Generally, agencies have written policies that govern disciplinary and adverse actions. These actions can range from oral admonishments, to written letters of reprimand, and to suspension, termination or removal actions. These policies also often put time limits on maintaining documentation of specific actions. The term "official discipline" should be understood as a disciplinary action that results in the placement of a document in an employee's official personnel file (OPF). In OPM's view, the bar on participation would remain in effect as long as the document stays in the employee's OPF. For example, an admonishment or reprimand usually comes out of the file after one or two years, respectively. However, a suspension and termination never come out of the file. Based on this reasoning and in this context, suspension and termination actions (**i.e., that are specifically related to the two categories of employees described in the law as ineligible**) which result in a document that permanently remains in the OPF would translate to a permanent prohibition on telework participation.

While each manager should remember that the intent of the Act is to promote and encourage telework, employees should understand that participation is not a "right;" rather, it should be based upon sound business and performance management principles.

Effective performance management is a key component of a successful telework program. The Act specifies in Section 6502(b)(3) that an agency's telework policy shall "provide that an employee may not be authorized to telework if the performance of that employee does not comply with the terms of the written agreement between the agency manager and that employee."

Participation also may be limited because of the duties encompassed by the position. Some positions are not conducive to telework, for example, positions involving sensitive materials and those requiring daily face-to-face contact. Remember, according to the Act, the agency's policy shall "ensure that telework does not diminish employee performance or agency operations." 5 U.S.C. 6502(b)(1). Furthermore, Section 6502(b)(4) states that telework participation would "not apply to any employee of the agency whose official duties require on a daily basis (every work day) (A) direct handling of secure materials determined to be inappropriate for telework by the agency head; or (B) on-site activity that cannot be handled remotely or at an alternate worksite . . . ."

When making determinations regarding employee participation, OPM strongly encourages agencies and managers to be creative in considering the use of telework and other workplace flexibilities. For example, many share the perception that telework is an "all or none" proposition, i.e., some managers believe the duties of a specific class of employees by their nature are simply not conducive to telework. Therefore, they dismiss outright the possibility of telework for those employees. However, this is not necessarily the case. Most, if not all, jobs include some duties that are considered to be "portable" in that they generally can be performed at any location. Examples of portable work are reading reports; analyzing documents and studies; preparing written letters, memorandums, reports and other correspondence; setting up conference calls, and similar tasks that do not necessarily require that an employee be physically present at the regular worksite.

In many positions, employees typically perform portable duties on a regular basis. These jobs tend to lend themselves to routine telework arrangements in which telework occurs as part of an ongoing, regular schedule. The degree of portability of an employee's work factors into determining how often the employee may be permitted to telework on a routine basis each pay period. In other cases, as indicated above, the nature of a position may make it appear that it is not conducive to telework. However, agencies and managers are encouraged to consider if certain portions of the employees' work are, in fact, consistent with the "portable" types of duties that lend themselves to telework.

For example, an employee may be in a clerical/receptionist position in which the majority of the duties usually must be performed on site, e.g., meeting and greeting visitors to the office on most days. However, this same employee will still have work days when reports must be written or electronic filing must be done. Is it possible that the employee can accomplish the latter work one or more days per pay period using a telework arrangement? A similar situation may involve law enforcement employees that are required to file paperwork or produce reports. Remember that the Act describes barriers to participation only in cases in which the employee's official duties fall outside what is conducive to telework **"every work day"** [Section 6502(b)(4)]. This means managers have flexibility to work out telework arrangements that take advantage of those days in which the employee is performing portable duties. Consistent with the Act, this flexible approach may open up the possibility for telework on a regular and recurring basis, even for positions previously thought to be ineligible.

Of course, there will be instances when a manager has made a good faith effort to accommodate telework for certain employees and simply cannot due to the nature of the work. In those cases, sound work/life principles and best practices would suggest that managers work with affected employees to avail them of opportunities to use workplace flexibilities appropriate to their situation, e.g., alternative work schedules such as flexible work schedules or compressed work schedules, etc.

Training

Agencies must ensure that "an interactive telework training program is provided to employees eligible to participate in the telework program of the agency; and all managers of teleworkers...," according to the law. The Act requires that "an employee has successfully completed the interactive telework training program before that employee enters into a written agreement to telework..." While agencies may provide their own telework training program for employees, OPM has offered and will continue to provide basic telework training modules (Telework 101) for employees and managers on www.telework.gov. As needed, OPM reviews these modules to update the information and to enhance the format and learning experience for participants.

Agencies will sometimes ask about the meaning of the term "interactive" in the context of the law. Does this mean that training must be "instructor-led" or face-to-face rather than via computer? In fact, the Act does not define the term "interactive," thereby leaving it subject to interpretation. OPM has always considered the Telework 101 training on the website (and therefore, online) to meet the definition of "interactive" in that there is a built-in opportunity for the trainee to self-assess his/her understanding through the use of frequent questions and answers and progress checks throughout. In addition, in 2011, OPM engaged in a project to enhance this training in a number of ways, including both substance and format. This was accomplished keeping in mind the need to improve "interactivity" through the selective use of media tools to make the training more engaging for employees. However, OPM's interpretation is that there is no requirement that this training be instructor-led as compared to via computer, i.e., Internet-based.

In many cases, agencies have employees with written agreements who have been teleworking for some time. In that case, are they still required to take the training? Not necessarily. The Act states that the head of the agency may provide for an exemption from the training requirements "if the head of the agency determines that the training would be unnecessary because the employee is already teleworking under a work arrangement in effect before the date of enactment..." The bottom line is that employees who have already been teleworking may be exempted from this training requirement; however, the decision to waive this requirement must be made by the agency head and implemented in the manner in which that is normally done in your agency. Even if employees are specifically exempted, OPM recommends that agencies provide to those employees at least updated information related to the Act since their original training would not have covered its requirements.

Agencies should also be aware that specialized training for managers is available through OPM's Eastern and Western Management Development Centers. Details on the Management Development Centers and course schedules can be found at www.leadership.opm.gov.

Telework Agreements

The Act **requires every telework participant to have a written agreement (regardless of whether telework is regular and recurring, or situational).** The written agreement is "entered into between an agency manager and an employee authorized to telework...outlines the specific work arrangement that is agreed to; and is **mandatory in order for any employee to participate in telework.**" It is important to remember that the Act requires that an employee successfully complete telework training before being allowed to enter into a written agreement and telework.

An employee may request a telework arrangement either orally or in writing (e.g., if an employee approaches her supervisor to participate in situational telework in order to complete a special project at home); however, this presumes that every employee has already successfully completed telework training and has a written telework agreement in place. It is especially important to take this into account for any employee that anticipates opting for "unscheduled telework" in accordance with dismissal and closure procedures. In other words, if an employee does not have a written telework agreement in place, that employee may not opt for "unscheduled telework" when it is offered due to the status of Federal Government operations. With this in mind, managers are strongly encouraged to think through potential employee situations and be flexible when developing telework agreements. For example, let's assume an employee is not likely to work a routine telework schedule but the person's duties would allow situational telework on a case-by-case basis. If the manager of the office anticipates the employee could potentially request "unscheduled telework" when offered during inclement weather, it is up to the manager and employee to agree on and sign a written telework agreement that stipulates the employee's eligibility for situational telework (which includes "unscheduled telework"). In addition, the employee should be encouraged to telework on an ad-hoc basis during the year to ensure s/he is prepared for such an eventuality.

Many agency policies and collective bargaining agreements currently describe specific requirements for the telework agreement, or make agreement templates available to employees and managers. For agencies seeking to develop or revise agreement forms, it might be helpful for you to consider this bulleted outline when drafting specific content. The following are recommended tips based on best practices in order to help guide you in this process; *they are not specifically required in the Act*:

➢ Term of the agreement: consider a one-year renewable agreement, or even a six-month agreement in telework situations that may need to be revised more frequently

➢ Type of telework specified by the agreement: describe if the agreement is for regular, recurring telework, or situational/ad-hoc/episodic telework

➢ Schedule: specify days of the week and the hours to be worked during telework days

➢ Requirements: outline any additional requirements (e.g., technology) beyond the prerequisites to telework outlined in the Act (e.g., training, written agreement)

- Expectations: clarify any assumptions, for example, regarding work location (e.g., if expected to work only from home) and frequency and modes of communication (e.g., email vs. telephone, core hours for contact, speed for returning calls)

- Equipment and other expenses: determine and specify equipment and/or expenses that will be covered by the agency, employee, or shared

- Expectations for emergency telework, i.e., be clear on whether or not an employee is expected to work in the case of a continuity event such as a National or local emergency; during an emergency event involving inclement weather; or another situation that may result in a disruption to normal office operations. With regard to Continuity of Operations, note that Emergency Relocation Group (ERG) members must be prepared to telework at any time.

- Information security: provide a summary for data security procedures in the agreement

- Safety: provide a self-certification safety checklist to telework employees as a guide when preparing the alternative work location for telework

- Termination/modification: ensure that employees know the agreement can be terminated or modified, and outline the conditions for termination/modification.

To summarize, telework agreements should be well-written, jargon-free, practical, and clear regarding responsibilities, roles and expectations. In short, written agreements should reflect and be consistent with the agency's telework policy.

Telework Managing Officer (TMO)

The Act requires that each agency designate a single position to function as a TMO. The TMO designation is new with the passage of the Act, which requires the TMO to be a senior official of the agency, established within the office of the Chief Human Capital Officer (CHCO), or its equivalent, and who has direct access to the head of the agency. Note that s/he does not need to be the CHCO. The important thing is that the position be given direct access to the head of the agency. The TMO is meant to be a strategic thinker and planner who will help the agency to incorporate telework in a way that makes good business sense.

The fact that someone is designated as the TMO does not mean that the individual who serves in this capacity is prohibited from holding another office or position in the agency. However, this person is directly accountable for the telework program at each agency.

The TMO:

- is responsible for policy development and implementation related to agency telework programs

- serves as an advisor for agency leadership, including the CHCO

- serves as a resource for managers and employees on telework matters

- is the primary point of contact with OPM on telework matters.

In addition to making telework an integral way of doing business in the agency, the TMO is responsible to help with the development of goals and metrics in order to evaluate the effectiveness of the program. In designating a TMO, agencies should look for the same leadership competencies and high standards that they would consider in selecting for any leadership position.

The way agencies implemented telework before the law was passed was that each agency had a "Telework Coordinator" at the Department/Agency level (e.g., Department of Homeland Security), and also individual "telework coordinators" at the subagency/subcomponent level (e.g., Immigration and Customs Enforcement, Transportation Security Administration, etc.). Whenever OPM would require agency-wide information on telework such as for the annual aggregate data collected on telework participation, it would work with the single point of contact at the Department/Agency-level. The Agency-wide coordinator would then work with his/her subcomponent "coordinators" to gather the information for their respective areas and then would tally everything to submit the data in a single report to OPM on behalf of the entire agency.

The TMO assumes many of the duties of what was formerly the Department-level "Telework Coordinator." The role within an agency of pulling together information on telework from various internal sources and then reporting to OPM now falls on the TMO. However, the TMO is much more than that since his/her duties extend beyond operational day-to-day aspects of telework and delve more into policy, advising, and an overarching management of the entire telework program for his/her agency.

Agencies have discretion as to whether or not, or how, they will continue to utilize "telework coordinators" to implement the day-to-day aspects of telework subject to the oversight of the TMO. The bottom line, however, is that **each agency will have only one individual, i.e., the TMO, who is the single accountable person according to the law for the agency's telework program**. In other words, when OPM contacts any given agency in the future to either request or disseminate information on Federal telework, we will contact the TMO. It will then be up to the TMO to coordinate internally with other staff members assisting with operational telework issues in that agency. Human Resource staff or agency employees that have questions or issues about telework should be encouraged to direct their concerns to the agency's TMO or the TMO's designee.

Reporting

Each year, OPM prepares and submits a report to the Congress that addresses the telework programs of each agency. This annual collaboration often begins with a Call for Telework Data from OPM to the agencies and culminates in the *Status of Telework in the Federal Government Report to the Congress*. The first report is due 18 months from the date of enactment of the law (approximately June 2012), and every year thereafter.

The report includes various types of information important to understanding agency progress in their telework programs including:

➢ the degree of participation by employees of each agency in teleworking during the period covered by the report (for some agencies, this will also include the degree of participation by bureau, division, or other major administrative unit)

➢ the method for gathering telework data in each agency

➢ the reasons for positive or negative variations in telework participation if the total number of employees teleworking is 10% higher or lower than the previous year in any agency

➢ the agency goal for increasing telework participation to the extent practicable or necessary

➢ an explanation of whether or not an agency met its goals for the last reporting period and, if not, what actions are being taken to identify and eliminate barriers

➢ an assessment of the progress each agency has made in meeting agency participation rate goals and other agency goals related to telework, such as the impact of telework on emergency readiness, energy use, recruitment and retention, performance, productivity, and employee attitudes and opinions regarding telework

➢ best practices in agency telework programs.

OPM will continue to work directly with the agency TMOs to discuss the types of data required and methods for data collection as the need arises.

Managers and Supervisors

This segment provides guidance to Federal managers and supervisors regarding their responsibilities under the Act to implement telework programs. Much of the above provided to Federal agencies and TMOs is directly applicable to managers and supervisors. Please consult the appropriate sections above for answers to many of your questions about implementing an effective telework program in your unit. In addition, please consider the following guidelines and tips.

How do Federal Managers and Supervisors Benefit from Telework?

Federal agencies, including managers and supervisors, can benefit from telework because it:

- helps with recruiting and retaining the best possible workforce
- ensures Continuity of Operations and maintains operations during emergency events - telework is a key component in ensuring the performance of essential Government functions during National or local emergencies such as natural disasters or National security incidents; or other situations that may disrupt normal operations
- promotes management effectiveness by targeting reductions in management costs related to employee turnover and absenteeism, and reduces real estate costs, transit costs, and environmental impact
- enhances work/life effectiveness and balance - telework allows employees to better manage their work and family obligations, thereby retaining a more resilient, results-oriented Federal workforce better able to meet agency mission and goals.

How to Be an Effective Manager or Supervisor of Teleworkers

Managerial and supervisory skill, participation and support can make telework an effective tool and asset for any organization. To effectively implement a telework program, managers should put the following guidelines, recommendations, and in some cases - laws, into practice.

Lead by Example - Managers and supervisors must be committed to using telework to the fullest extent possible if Federal telework programs are to succeed. Research in the work/life field bears out that supervisors, managers and senior executives who model the use of workplace flexibilities such as telework in any organization serve as key drivers in effecting positive cultural change in that organization. This is especially so if the organization's climate and culture have traditionally reflected a skeptical, or even hostile, view of telework. There is a tendency for employees to model the behavior of supervisors. Non-participation of supervisors may send a non-verbal message of disapproval. It might even suggest that getting ahead in the Federal workforce (e.g., being promoted) depends on the employee's physical presence at the main worksite. Managers and supervisors that telework will help to dispel this false notion and lead the way towards a telework-friendly culture in the agency.

Know Your Telework Managing Officer (TMO) - Each agency has designated a TMO who serves as the primary point of contact for policy and program questions. Managers should maintain frequent contact with their TMO, or the TMO's designee, to ensure the agency's policy and procedures are properly applied and to ensure they are aware of the full range of support and resources available to them.

Know Your Telework Policy and Procedures, Including Applicable Collective Bargaining Agreements - Managers should familiarize themselves and their employees with their agency's policy and applicable collective bargaining agreements to ensure they are in compliance with their requirements. Most agency policies and many collective bargaining agreements will include procedures for establishing telework agreements, obtaining equipment, and related matters.

In addition, all agencies should have policies on information systems and technology security (see the section on **Safety** below), and managers/supervisors must ensure their equipment choices and telework agreements comply with these policies. Information security includes protection of sensitive "hard-copy" files and documents.

Participate in Training - As described above, OPM offers online interactive telework training for managers and employees at www.telework.gov. It can be accessed directly at the following link: www.telework.gov/tools_and_resources/training/index.aspx. Also, many agencies offer their own telework training and TMOs are available to consult with managers. Remember that employees who wish to telework must successfully complete telework training prior to entering into a written telework agreement, unless exempted by the head of the agency as provided in the law [P.L. 111-292, Section 6503(b)]. Managers and supervisors are encouraged to complete telework training.

Information technology security training, administered at the agency level, is mandatory. Managers must ensure teleworkers complete this training and understand their responsibilities in safeguarding work-related information.

Determine Employee Eligibility - Agencies have discretion to determine telework eligibility criteria for their employees, subject to the requirements and limitations of the law. These criteria should be detailed in agency policy and may also be covered in applicable collective bargaining agreements. See the section on **Eligibility and Participation** above for guidelines on making these types of determinations based on the law and your agency's telework policy.

Understand and Assess the Needs of the Group - Telework is often implemented piecemeal, rather than strategically, as individuals request arrangements. This reactive approach carries the risk of raising fairness issues. To the extent possible, telework should be implemented strategically, taking into account the needs and work of the group. Agencies have made this easier by making broader determinations on employee eligibility and notifying employees. However, managers and supervisors may be making decisions with regard to situational telework and groups of newly-hired employees.

Create and Sign Written Telework Agreements - The teleworker and his or her manager/supervisor must enter into a written telework agreement for every type of telework, whether the employee teleworks regularly or on a situational basis. The parameters of this agreement are most often laid out by the agency policy and/or collective bargaining agreement, but should include certain key elements (reference the Act or the section above on **Telework Agreements**). Most importantly, the agreement should be signed and dated by the manager and employee. Managers and TMOs are encouraged to keep copies of all telework agreements on file.

Telework agreements are living documents and should be revisited by the manager and teleworker and re-signed regularly, preferably at regular intervals as defined by your agency's telework policy and applicable collective bargaining agreements. At a minimum, new telework agreements should be prepared and signed when a new employee/supervisory relationship is established.

OPM strongly recommends that agencies include specific language in the telework agreement for any employee who may potentially be asked to telework in case of emergency situations or continuity events. Continuity events would include a National or local emergency or pandemic health crisis that results in activation of continuity plans. Emergency events would include inclement weather or other situations that may disrupt normal operations and lead to an offering of "unscheduled telework." Remember that the law requires all teleworkers to have a written telework agreement in place. This means that an employee who wishes to opt for "unscheduled telework" during a weather emergency may not telework if a written agreement is not in place. Individuals that are potential situational teleworkers (including "unscheduled telework") should be encouraged to practice teleworking on a regular basis and as often as possible.

Base Denials on Business Reasons - Telework requests may be denied and telework agreements may be terminated. Telework is not an employee right, even if the employee is considered "telework-eligible."

Denial and termination decisions must be based on operational needs or performance in accordance with the description in the law, not personal reasons. For example, a manager may deny a telework arrangement if the duties of the position are not amenable to telework. If the employee's denial or termination was as a result of a performance issue, the denial or termination should include information about when the employee might reapply, and also if applicable, what actions the employee should take to improve his or her chance of approval. Denials should be provided in a timely manner. Managers should also review the agency's collective bargaining agreement(s) and telework policy to ensure they meet any applicable requirements.

Managers should provide employees (and keep copies of) signed written denials or terminations of telework agreements. These should include information about why the arrangement was denied or terminated. The TMO should also be alerted regarding denials or terminations and copies provided to him/her as well.

With respect to employees covered by a collective bargaining agreement, appeals will be governed by the negotiated grievance procedure (unless this subject is specifically excluded from that procedure by the collective bargaining agreement, in which case the agency grievance procedure would govern). For non-bargaining unit employees, the agency grievance procedure in force would cover appeals from a denial of a request to telework.

Use Good Performance Management Practices - It is important to note that performance standards for teleworking employees must be the same as performance standards for non-teleworking employees. Management expectations for performance should be clearly addressed in the employee's performance plan, and the performance plan should be reviewed to ensure the standards do not create inequities or inconsistencies between teleworking and non-teleworking employees. Like non-teleworking employees, teleworkers are held accountable for the results they produce. Good performance management techniques practiced by a manager will mean a smooth, easier transition to a telework environment. Resources for performance management are available from OPM at www.opm.gov/perform.

Communicate Expectations - The telework agreement provides a framework for the discussion that needs to take place between the manager and the employee about expectations. For all types of telework, this discussion is important to ensure that managers and employees understand one another's expectations concerning basic issues such as the following:

➢ What technologies will be used to maintain contact?

➢ What equipment will the agency provide; what equipment will the teleworker provide; what will be shared?

➢ Who provides technical assistance in the event of equipment disruption?

➢ What will the weekly/monthly telework schedule be?

➢ How will the manager and co-workers be kept updated about the schedule?

➢ Do changes need to be pre-approved?

➢ What will the daily telework schedule be; will the hours be the same as in the main office, or will they be different?

➢ What are the physical attributes of the telework office and do they conform to basic safety standards? (agencies may wish to provide employees with a self-certifying safety checklist for guidance)

➢ What are the expectations for availability by phone, email, etc?

➢ What is the expectation regarding the amount of notice (if any) given for reporting to the official worksite, and how will such notice be provided?

➢ How is a telework agreement terminated by management or the employee?

➢ Who is expected to telework in an emergency?

➢ What is expected of a teleworker in the event of an emergency?

Facilitate Communication with All Members of the Work Group - Teleworking and non-teleworking employees must understand expectations regarding telework arrangements including coverage, communication and responsibilities. Although individual teleworkers must take responsibility for their own availability and information sharing, managers can help ensure that methods are in place to maintain open communication across the members of a work group. Employees and managers alike are encouraged to exercise professional courtesy in keeping one another informed about their availability throughout the work day.

Maintain Fairness in Assigning Work and Rewarding Performance - Managers should avoid distributing work based on "availability" as measured by physical presence, and avoid the pitfall of assuming someone who is present and looks busy is actually accomplishing more work than someone who is off-site. Good performance management practices are essential for telework to be effective and equitable.

Make Good Decisions About Equipment - GSA offers guidelines for the equipment and support an agency may provide to teleworkers, in Federal Management Regulation (FMR) Bulletin 2006-B3, Guidelines for Alternative Workplace Arrangements (see "GSA Telework Information" in the **References** section at the end of this document). Generally, decisions regarding the ways in which teleworkers should be equipped are made by the agency and individual manager consistent with the agency's telework policy and applicable collective bargaining agreements. Managers should familiarize themselves with these guidelines and also with their agency's policy on equipment. Within those constraints, the challenge for managers is in finding the right balance between budget, security and effectiveness. Factors to consider include technology needs based on the work of the employee, agency security requirements, and budget constraints. In addition, managers may also need to have conversations as appropriate to ensure the availability of equipment related to requests for reasonable accommodation.

Practice Telework - The success of an organization's telework program depends on regular, routine use. Experience is the only way to enable managers, employees, information technology (IT) support, and other stakeholders to work through any technology, equipment, communications, workflow, and associated issues that may inhibit the transparency of telework. Individuals expected or anticipated to telework in an emergency situation, including managers and supervisors, should be encouraged to telework with some frequency under non-emergency circumstances. Managers and supervisors should make it a point to regularly participate in telework in order to lead by example and be comfortable in dealing with the dynamics of managing in a telework environment.

Safety - Teleworkers must address issues of their own personal safety to be effective while teleworking from a home office or other alternative worksite. Government employees causing or suffering work-related injuries and/or damages at the alternative worksite are covered by the Military Personnel and Civilian Employees Claims Act, the Federal Tort Claims Act, or the Federal Employees' Compensation Act (workers' compensation), as appropriate.

Managers should review a safety checklist with teleworkers to ensure compliance and should immediately investigate any reports of accidents or injuries on the job.

Employees

This segment provides guidance to employees regarding their participation in agency telework programs. Employees should be aware of the information on telework provided to Federal agencies and TMOs above. Please consult the appropriate sections above for answers to many of your questions about your agency's telework program in the context of the law. In addition, please consider the following guidelines and tips.

Why Would I Want to Participate in Telework?

Employees may benefit from telework because:

➢ it helps employees have greater flexibility in accomplishing their work while also meeting personal and community responsibilities

➢ it can help reduce stress by decreasing commuting time, freeing that time up to accomplish family and personal matters

➢ it can help free you from office distractions, which may be particularly important when working on a complex project

➢ it encourages engagement in your agency - when employees feel they have greater control over their work environment, they tend to feel more committed to their organizations.

How to Be an Effective Teleworker

Employees who understand the responsibilities and expectations for all parties involved will have a more successful experience with telework. To be an effective teleworker, employees should put the following guidelines, recommendations, and in some cases - laws, into practice.

Know Your Telework Managing Officer (TMO) - Each agency has designated a TMO who serves as the primary point of contact for policy and program questions. Employees should maintain contact with their TMO or the TMO's designee for support and assistance as well as to ensure they follow the agency's policy and procedures.

Know Your Telework Policy and Procedures, Including Applicable Collective Bargaining Agreements - Employees should familiarize themselves with their agency's policy. and applicable collective bargaining agreements to ensure they are in compliance with their requirements. Most agency policies will include procedures for establishing telework agreements, obtaining equipment, and related matters.

In addition, all agencies should have policies on information systems and technology security (see **Safety**), and employees should work with their managers/supervisors to ensure their equipment choices and telework agreements comply with these policies. Information security includes protection of sensitive "hard-copy" files and documents needed for work.

Conduct a Self-Assessment - A successful telework arrangement begins with a good self-assessment. Employees should consider the following factors in making an honest determination about their telework capabilities:

➢ My duties include sufficient "portable" work for the amount of telework being proposed

➢ I have the ability to work independently, without close supervision

➢ I am comfortable with technology needed (if any) to telework

➢ I have good communication with my supervisor, co-workers, and customers that will enable a relatively seamless transition from my official site to my alternative site

➢ I have sufficient telework office space at my alternative location in order to get work done

➢ My work area is safe and meets all agency telework policy requirements for safety

➢ Dependent care arrangements (e.g., child care, elder care, or care of any dependent adults) are in place because I recognize that I may not use telework as a means for dependent care

➢ I have the ability to be flexible about the telework arrangement in order to respond to the needs of the supervisor, work group, and the work load.

Participate in Training - As described above, OPM offers online interactive telework training for managers and employees at www.telework.gov. It can be accessed directly at the following link: www.telework.gov/tools_and_resources/training/index.aspx. Also, many agencies offer their own telework training. Remember that employees who wish to telework must successfully complete telework training prior to entering into a written telework agreement, unless exempted by the head of the agency as provided in the law [P.L. 111-292, Section 6503(b)].

Information technology security training, administered at the agency level, is also mandatory. Teleworkers must complete this training and understand their responsibilities in safeguarding work-related information.

Enter into A Signed, Written Telework Agreement - The teleworker and his or her manager/supervisor must enter into a written telework agreement for every type of telework, whether the employee teleworks regularly or on a situational basis. The parameters of this agreement are most often laid out by the agency policy and/or collective bargaining agreement, but should include certain key elements (reference the Act or the section above on **Telework Agreements**). Most importantly, the agreement should be signed and dated by the manager and employee.
Elements that should be incorporated into a written telework agreement include:

➢ the location of the telework office (typically the home residence of the employee)

➢ an equipment inventory, i.e., what the employee will supply; what the agency will supply, what will be shared

➢ the telework schedule

- telework contact information (e.g., the phone number to use on the telework day)
- a safety checklist, i.e., a self-certifying list to guide you in checking the safety of your alternative work site
- expectations for emergency telework, i.e., be clear on whether or not you are expected to work in the case of a continuity event such as a National or local emergency; during an emergency event involving inclement weather; or another situation that may result in a disruption to normal office operations. With regard to Continuity of Operations, note that Emergency Relocation Group (ERG) members must be prepared to telework at any time.

Telework agreements need to be updated as circumstances change, e.g., if the telework schedule changes. The manager and teleworker should work together periodically to evaluate the arrangement, make changes in the agreement as necessary, and re-sign the document.

Safeguard Information and Data - Employees must take responsibility for the security of the data and other information they handle while teleworking. Employees should:

- be familiar with, understand, and comply with their agency's information security policies
- participate in agency information security training; and
- maintain security of any relevant materials, including files, correspondence, and equipment, in addition to following security protocols for remote connectivity. Depending on the sensitivity of the information being handled, the home office may need to include security measures such as locked file cabinets, similar to what may be used at the official worksite.

Plan the Work - Employees who telework should assess the portability of their work and the level of technology available at the remote site as they prepare for telework. Employees are encouraged to plan their telework days to be as productive as possible by considering the following questions:

- What files or other documents will I need to take with me when I leave my main worksite the day before teleworking?
- What equipment will I need to take?
- Who needs to be notified that I will be teleworking?
- What other steps should I take before I leave my office (e.g., forwarding the phone)?
- In the case of emergency or "unscheduled" telework, what should I have available at all times at my alternative worksite to enable me to be functional without going back to the main office to retrieve materials?

<u>Manage Expectations and Communication</u> - Managers are ultimately responsible for the effective functioning of the work group. Nevertheless, teleworkers should help manage the group's expectations and their own communication to avoid any negative impact from their arrangement. Issues that should be addressed include the following:

➢ Backup - even with very portable work there are invariably instances where physical presence is required and a co-worker may need to step in. Co-worker backup should be planned, it should not be onerous, and it should be reciprocal. Cross-training of staff has broad organizational benefits and should be a management priority

➢ On-the-spot Assistance - teleworkers may occasionally need someone who is physically present in the main office to assist them (e.g., to fax a document or look up information). Again, these arrangements should not be unduly burdensome; a "buddy system" between teleworkers may be the least disruptive solution

➢ Communication with the Manager - the manager must be kept apprised of the teleworker's schedule, how to make contact with the teleworker, and the status of all pending work

➢ Communication with Co-workers and Customers - co-workers must be informed about the appropriate handling of telephone calls or other communications that are the teleworker's responsibility, and customers should not notice that the teleworker is working from an alternative worksite (i.e., work should be seamless).

<u>Safety</u> - Teleworkers must address issues of their own personal safety to be effective while teleworking from a home office or other alternative worksite. Government employees causing or suffering work-related injuries and/or damages at the alternative worksite are covered by the Military Personnel and Civilian Employees Claims Act, the Federal Tort Claims Act, or the Federal Employees' Compensation Act (workers' compensation), as appropriate.

Employees should:

➢ provide appropriate telework space, with ergonomically correct chair, desk, and computer equipment

➢ complete a safety checklist self-certifying the space is free from hazards. This checklist is not legally binding, but details management expectations and, if signed, assumes compliance

➢ immediately report any work-related accident occurring at the telework site and provide the supervisor with all medical documentation related to the accident. It may be necessary for an agency representative to access the home office to investigate the report.

ADDITIONAL GUIDANCE

Safety

Federal agencies and staff are responsible for the security of Federal Government property, information, and information systems. Telework does not change this responsibility. If not properly implemented, telework may introduce vulnerabilities into agency systems and networks. To prevent security incidents, the Federal Information Security Management Act of 2002 requires agencies to protect information and information systems commensurate with risk. In addition, OMB memorandum M-06-16 recommends actions to protect remote information that all agencies should continue to implement. Agencies should refer to the NIST security telework site for more information at http://csrc.nist.gov/telework.

Performance Management

Effective performance management is important to the success of the telework program. The Act specifies in Section 6502(b)(3) that an agency's telework policy shall "provide that an employee may not be authorized to telework if the performance of that employee does not comply with the terms of the written agreement between the agency manager and that employee." When agencies make decisions regarding telework eligibility and participation, sound business and performance management principles must be considered, consistent with the requirements of the Act.

When implementing the telework program, managers should keep in mind that performance standards for teleworking employees must be the same as performance standards for non-teleworking employees. Also, management expectations for performance should be clearly addressed in an employee's performance plan, regardless of whether or not the employee is a teleworker. When an employee participates in telework, expectations related to accountability do not differ by virtue of the telework arrangement. Following clear and consistent performance management principles and techniques should result in a seamless transition for managers and their employees moving to telework arrangements. Resources for performance management are available from OPM at www.opm.gov/perform.

Pay, Leave and Work Schedule Flexibilities

Pay

An employee's pay is based on the location of the employee's official duty station (worksite). An agency must determine and designate the official worksite for an employee covered by a telework agreement on a case-by-case basis using the following criteria:

➢ the official worksite for an employee covered by a telework agreement is the location of the regular worksite for the employee's position (i.e., the place where the employee would normally work absent a telework agreement), as long as the employee is scheduled to report physically at least twice each bi-weekly pay period on a regular and recurring basis to that regular worksite

➢ the official worksite for an employee covered by a telework agreement who is not scheduled to report at least twice each bi-weekly pay period on a regular and recurring basis to the regular worksite is the location of the telework site (i.e., home or other alternative worksite), except in certain temporary situations

➢ in the case of a telework employee whose work location varies on a recurring basis, the employee need not report at least twice each bi-weekly pay period to the regular worksite established by the agency as long as the employee is performing work within the same geographic area (established for the purpose of a given pay entitlement) as the employee's regular worksite. For example, if a telework employee with a varying work location works at least twice each bi-weekly pay period on a regular and recurring basis in the same locality pay area in which the established official worksite is located, the employee need not report at least twice each bi-weekly pay period to that official worksite to maintain entitlement to the locality payment for that area.

Pay During Temporary Telework Arrangements

In certain temporary situations, an agency may designate the location of the regular worksite as the official worksite of an employee who teleworks on a regular basis at an alternative worksite, even though the employee is not able to report at least twice each bi-weekly pay period on a regular and recurring basis to the regular worksite.

➢ the intent of this exception is to address certain situations where the employee is retaining a residence in the commuting area for the regular worksite but is temporarily unable to report to the regular worksite for reasons beyond the employee's control

➢ a key consideration is the need to preserve equity between the telework employee and non-telework employees who are working in the same area as the telework location. Also, the temporary exception should generally be used only in cases where (1) the employee is expected to stop teleworking and return to work at the regular worksite in the near future, or (2) the employee is expected to continue teleworking but will be able to report to the regular worksite at least twice each bi-weekly pay period on a regular and recurring basis in the near future.

For more information on official duty station, please see
http://www.opm.gov/oca/pay/HTML/Official_Duty_Station.asp.

Premium Pay

Typically, the same premium pay rules apply to employees who telework versus those who report in to their regular worksites.

➤ *Night Pay* - Night pay is a 10 percent differential paid to employees for ***regularly scheduled work*** performed at night. It is computed as a percentage of the employee's rate of basic pay (including any applicable locality payment or special rate supplement) (emphasis added). A teleworker may not earn night pay by choosing to work at night. Night pay is paid for regularly scheduled work performed at night. This generally means work scheduled before the beginning of the administrative workweek. However, night pay is also paid for night work on a temporary assignment to a different daily tour of duty <u>during</u> the administrative workweek.

Please see http://www.opm.gov/oca/pay/html/NIGHT.asp for more information on night pay.

➤ *Sunday Premium Pay* - An employee is entitled to 25 percent of his or her rate of basic pay for work performed during a ***regularly scheduled*** basic 8-hour tour of duty that begins or ends on a Sunday (emphasis added). A teleworker must be regularly scheduled to work on a Sunday in order for that employee to be eligible for the 25 percent Sunday premium pay.

Please see http://www.opm.gov/oca/WORKSCH/HTML/sunday.htm for more information on Sunday premium pay.

Leave and Work Scheduling Flexibilities

An employee must follow his/her agency's telework policy for requesting leave and work scheduling changes when teleworking.

Similar to when an employee is at his or her regular worksite, an employee can take leave for a portion of the day. Agencies may choose to allow an employee to adjust his/her work schedule during a telework day based on the employee's telework agreement (e.g., to attend a medical appointment or deal with a household repair). Both leave and work scheduling flexibilities are not only to assist the employee in balancing his or her personal needs, but also to maintain productivity by allowing the employee to work around disruption in his or her work day.

For additional information on leave administration, please visit http://www.opm.gov/oca/leave/index.asp.

For additional information on pay administration, premium pay, and work scheduling, please visit http://www.opm.gov/oca/pay/HTML/factindx.asp.

Telework and Continuity of Operations

The Act states that "each executive agency shall incorporate telework into the continuity of operations plan of that agency." Federal Continuity Directive (FCD) 1, *National Continuity Program and Requirements,* U.S. Department of Homeland Security, February 2008 (http://www.fema.gov/about/org/ncp/coop/planning.shtm), defines COOP as "an effort within individual agencies to ensure they can continue to perform their Mission Essential Functions (MEFs) and Primary Mission Essential Functions (PMEFs) during a wide range of emergencies, including localized acts of nature, accidents, and technological or attack-related emergencies."

There is a direct relationship between the Continuity of Operations (COOP) plan and telework. The two programs, telework and COOP, share a basic objective: to perform and maintain agency functions from an alternative location. Telework can help ensure that essential Federal functions continue during emergency situations.

Telework must be a part of all agency emergency planning. Telework allows employees to conduct some or all of their work at an alternative worksite away from the employee's typically used office since that may not be viable during an emergency. Each Department and Agency is encouraged to conduct an annual telework exercise where employees participate in a telework day, in order to test the organization's capability.

Management must be committed to implementing telework as broadly as possible to take full advantage of the potential of telework for this purpose and ensure that:

> equipment, technology, and technical support have been tested

> employees practice telework so that they are comfortable with the technology and communications methods

> managers practice telework so that they are comfortable managing a distributed workgroup

The key to successful use of telework in the event of an emergency is an effective routine telework program. An agency's telework policy should include:

> information on who is expected to telework in an emergency
> what is expected of teleworkers in the event of an emergency.

As many employees as possible should have telework capability that includes:

> having a telework agreement in place
> connectivity
> equipment commensurate with work needs
> ability to practice telework on a regular basis to ensure effectiveness during an emergency.

Manager Responsibilities

➢ Understand the agency's emergency plans (continuity plan, pandemic plan, etc.) and management roles in executing the plan

➢ Implement telework to the greatest extent possible so systems are in place to support successful telework in an emergency

➢ Notify employees designated as emergency personnel for a continuity or pandemic event

➢ Communicate expectations to both emergency and non-emergency employees regarding their roles and responsibilities in an emergency

➢ Establish communication processes to notify emergency employees and non-emergency employees of the activation of the agency's emergency plan and the agency operating status during the emergency

➢ Integrate emergency expectations into telework agreements as appropriate

➢ Determine how employees who telework will communicate with one another and with management to accomplish work

➢ Determine how time and attendance will be maintained

➢ Allow personnel who might telework in case of an emergency to telework regularly to ensure functionality.

Teleworker Responsibilities

➢ Maintain a current telework agreement detailing any emergency telework responsibilities specified for a continuity and/or pandemic event, as appropriate

➢ Practice telework regularly to ensure effectiveness

➢ Be familiar with the agency's emergency plans (continuity plan, pandemic plan, etc.) and your manager's expectations for how you will telework during such events

➢ Be flexible; be willing to perform all duties assigned to you by management even if they are outside your usual or customary duties.

Washington, DC, Area Dismissal and Closure Procedures
(Unscheduled Telework Option)

In 2010, OPM unveiled the unscheduled telework option as a way for agencies and employees to continue work operations during snow and other emergencies and ensure the safety of the Federal workforce. The unscheduled telework option is a type of situational, or ad-hoc telework, that will allow employees in the Washington, DC, area to work from home or a nearby alternative location, when OPM announces a modified operating status due to inclement weather or special events that severely impact commuting.

For example, when OPM announces that "Federal agencies in the Washington, DC, area are **OPEN** and employees have the **OPTION** for **UNSCHEDULED LEAVE OR UNSCHEDULED TELEWORK,**" eligible teleworkers will have the option of reporting to the office or notifying their supervisor of their intent to take unscheduled leave or perform unscheduled telework. The unscheduled leave and unscheduled telework options are also incorporated into other dismissal announcements. Agencies are encouraged to consult the OPM publication, *Washington, DC, Area Dismissal and Closure Procedures*, for answers to questions about dismissal or closure situations.

Recruitment and Retention

Federal agency recruitment and retention efforts are directly affected by the use of telework as a management tool and are addressed in the Act.

The implementation of the Act provides a unique opportunity to leverage telework as a human capital management tool. Managers are encouraged to use telework as a tool to help attract, recruit, and retain the best possible workforce. Many people seek jobs with an option to telework as a means to reduce commuting time and costs and improve their work/life effectiveness. Telework can broaden the pool of highly qualified candidates because it provides flexibilities that meet varying needs. For example, telework may be used as a reasonable accommodation for an individual with a disability who may require, or prefer, to work at home. While not all persons with disabilities need, or want, to work from home, telework provides a viable option for individuals with disabilities that affect mobility or pose related challenges. Additionally, telework allows employers to hire individuals who live further away from what would be considered a reasonable commuting distance from their place of employment and who are not able to relocate. It also helps employers retain top-performing employees who want or need to relocate their residence beyond the local commuting area.

Telework can also help managers in other ways. For example, it can be used as an effective succession planning tool. Telework is an appealing option for many retirees who are willing to continue working with their former organization, thereby helping to facilitate a smooth and continuous transition of institutional knowledge and technical competencies.

Accommodations for Employees with Disabilities

The flexible arrangements we describe as "telework" are governed by the telework laws, i.e., Public Law 106-346, § 359 (2000); Public Law 108-199, Division B, § 627 (2004); Public Law 108-447, Division B, § 622 (2004); and, most recently, Public Law 111-292 (the Telework Enhancement Act of 2010). Although an agency with a robust, well-functioning telework policy may find that such a policy also enhances the agency's ability to grant reasonable accommodations that work well for the agency and the persons with disabilities who request them alike, it is important that requests to telework be analyzed and evaluated under their appropriate scheme, i.e., the telework laws and that requests for reasonable accommodations be analyzed and evaluated under the statutory framework that applies to them.

Reasonable accommodations are governed by Section 501 of the Rehabilitation Act of 1973 (Rehabilitation Act), *as amended*, 29 U.S.C. § 791 *et seq.*, which was made applicable to Federal employees pursuant to the Americans with Disabilities Act. The Rehabilitation Act requires Federal employers to provide requested "reasonable accommodations" to employees with disabilities, unless to do so would cause an "undue hardship." The determination as to whether an employee may be granted the accommodation requested should be made through a flexible "interactive process" between the employer and the employee. Executive Order 13164, *Requiring Federal Agencies to Establish Procedures to Facilitate the Provision of Reasonable Accommodation*, requires all Federal agencies to develop a Reasonable Accommodation Policy. Therefore, agencies should refer to their Reasonable Accommodation Policy when considering reasonable accommodation requests. For example, depending upon the facts of a particular accommodation request, an agency that might have determined that a particular position should be ineligible for telework, might be required nevertheless to permit an employee with a disability within the meaning of the Rehabilitation Act to work from home to some degree. For more information on reasonable accommodation and the interactive process, see *The U.S. Equal Employment Opportunity Commission's (EEOC) Revised Enforcement Guidance: Reasonable Accommodation and Undue Hardship Under the Americans With Disabilities Act*, at http://www.eeoc.gov/policy/docs/accommodation.html. The EEOC has also provided guidance that focuses more specifically on the use of work from home as a reasonable accommodation in some circumstances. See the *Equal Employment Opportunity Commission (EEOC) Guidance on Work At Home/Telework as a Reasonable Accommodation*, at www.eeoc.gov/facts/telework.html, for more information.

It is important to distinguish between ordinary requests to telework and requests from persons with disabilities for reasonable accommodations and to know which is being requested in any given situation before attempting to analyze the request. If there is any ambiguity about what is being requested, managers and supervisors should clarify that ambiguity at the outset. It is often very fruitful for agency managers and supervisors to consult with the agency's reasonable accommodation manager and/or the agency's counsel as part of the interactive process established by the Rehabilitation Act, in order to fully understand managers' and supervisors' responsibilities under the law.

Reasonable Accommodation Financial Resources - The Department of Defense's Computer/Electronic Accommodations Program (CAP) supports agency reasonable accommodation processes by providing services and accommodations for employees with disabilities who work from home as a form of reasonable accommodation.

CAP's support includes evaluating the needs of employees with disabilities and purchasing the assistive devices and technology necessary to effectively complete their duties, whether on site or under a reasonable accommodation to work from home. This also serves as a retention strategy and reduces disability retirement costs and actions. For more information, contact CAP at www.tricare.mil/cap.

In addition, the Government-funded Job Accommodation Network (JAN) is a free service that offers employers and individuals ideas about effective accommodations. The counselors perform individualized searches for workplace accommodations based on a job's functional requirements, the functional limitations of the individual, environmental factors, and other pertinent information. JAN can be reached at 1-800-526-7234 (voice or TDD); or at www.jan.wvu.edu/soar.

Conclusion

This is an exciting time for Federal telework! By following the guidance in this document, agencies, managers, supervisors, and employees will be ahead of the game in improving their understanding and implementation of telework. The success realized through the widespread use of this important workplace flexibility will contribute to a more efficient, effective and resilient Federal workforce, and to the achievement of our ultimate objective of better service to our Nation.

REFERENCES

TELEWORK (GENERAL)

Telework Central Website (OPM in partnership with GSA)
www.telework.gov

GSA Telework Information
www.gsa.gov/portal/category/21272

WORKPLACE FLEXIBILITIES

White House Workplace Flexibility Report
www.whitehouse.gov/files/documents/100331-cea-economics-workplace-flexibility.pdf

Work Schedules and Workplace Flexibilities (OPM Information)
www.opm.gov/oca/worksch/INDEX.asp

TELEWORK LEGISLATION, REPORTS AND STUDIES

Legislation
www.telework.gov/guidance_and_legislation/telework_legislation/index.aspx

Reports and Studies
www.telework.gov/reports_and_studies/index.aspx

TELEWORK TRAINING

Training (OPM Telework 101)
www.telework.gov/tools_and_resources/training/index.aspx

Training (OPM Eastern and Western Management Development Centers)
https://www.leadership.opm.gov

PERFORMANCE MANAGEMENT
Performance Management
www.opm.gov/perform

RECORDS MANAGEMENT
National Archives and Records Administration's FAQs
http://www.archives.gov/faqs/

PAY AND LEAVE ADMINISTRATION

Pay Administration, Premium Pay and Work Scheduling
www.opm.gov/oca/pay/HTML/factindx.asp

Unscheduled Telework
www.opm.gov/oca/compmemo/dismissal.pdf

ACCOMMODATIONS FOR EMPLOYEES WITH DISABILITIES

EEOC Enforcement Guidance
www.eeoc.gov/policy/docs/accommodation.html

EEOC on Telework and Work at Home
www.eeoc.gov/facts/telework.html

Computer/Electronic Accommodations Program (CAP)
http://cap.tricare.mil

Job Accommodation Network
http://askjan.org

SAFETY (OMB, DHS and NIST)

http://csrc.nist.gov/telework

TELEWORK AND EMERGENCY PLANNING

FEMA COOP Information
www.fema.gov/about/org/ncp/coop

Federal Continuity Directive (FCD) 1
www.fema.gov/about/org/ncp/coop/planning.shtm

OPM Pandemic Planning Information
www.opm.gov/pandemic

www.ingramcontent.com/pod-product-compliance
Lightning Source LLC
Chambersburg PA
CBHW080633290526
45790CB00007B/3043